DEION SANDERS

PRIME TIME

By Miles Harvey

CP Children's Press®
A Division of Grolier Publishing
New York   London   Hong Kong   Sydney
Danbury, Connecticut

Photo Credits

Cover, AP/Wide World; 5, ©Rich Kane/Sports Chrome East/West; 6, ©Mitchell B. Reibel/Sports Photo Masters, Inc.; 9, ©Michael Ponzini/Focus on Sports; 12, 17, ©Allen Steele/AllSport; 18, ©Stephen Dunn/AllSport; 21, Sports Chrome East/West; 22, 25, AP/Wide World; 27, UPI Bettmann; 28, AP Wide World; 31 (left), ©Bill Hickey/AllSport; 31 (right), 32, Focus on Sports; 35, Sports Chrome East/West; 36, ©Jim Gund/AllSport; 37, ©Thearon Henderson/Focus on Sports; 38, ©Stephen Dunn/AllSport; 40, ©Rob Tringali, Jr./Sports Chrome East/West; 41, 43, AP/Wide World; 44 (left), ©Allen Steele/AllSport; 44 (right), ©Bill Hickey/AllSport; 45 (left), AP/Wide World; 45 (right), 46, ©Stephen Dunn/AllSport; 47, AP/Wide World

Editorial Staff

Project Editor: Mark Friedman
Design: Herman Adler Design Group
Photo Editor: Jan Izzo

Library of Congress Cataloging-in-Publication Data

Harvey, Miles.
    Deion Sanders : Prime Time / by Miles Harvey.
      p. cm. – (Sports stars)
    ISBN 0-516-04395-1
    1. Sanders, Deion—Juvenile literature. 2. Baseball players—United States—Biography—Juvenile literature. 3. Football players—United States—Biography—Juvenile literature. I. Title. II. Series.
GV865.S22H37   1996
796.357'092–dc20   95-40603
[B]   CIP
                                 AC

DEION SANDERS
PRIME TIME

The Los Angeles Rams punter kicked the ball high into the air. A young Atlanta Falcons player waited to catch it. His name was Deion Sanders, and he was very nervous. It was Deion's first game in the National Football League (NFL). He wanted to show the fans at Atlanta's Fulton County Stadium that he was a good player.

As the ball came down, Rams players charged toward Deion, ready to knock him to the ground. He reached out for the football, and he caught it . . . but then it fell to the ground! The crowd gasped in dismay, but Deion recovered. He picked up the ball and started to run. He broke one tackle, then another, and another. The fans screamed with excitement as Deion streaked down the field. He ran into the end zone.

Deion Sanders had been in the NFL only five minutes, and already he had scored a touchdown! But that was just one of his incredible feats that week. Five days earlier, Deion had hit a home run while playing baseball for the New York Yankees.

No other athlete ever had knocked a homer in major-league baseball and scored a touchdown in pro football in the same week. And Deion accomplished this as a rookie!

Since his rookie year in 1989, Deion has become even better at both football and baseball. Few athletes make the pros in one sport, but for several years, Deion was a star in two. He just may be the greatest two-sport athlete of all time.

Deion Luwynn Sanders was born on August 9, 1967. He grew up in Fort Myers, Florida. Things weren't always easy for Deion as a kid. His parents were divorced, and Deion's mother, Connie, didn't have much money. She had to work two jobs to support Deion and his sister, Tracie. But Connie gave her children a lot of love. "Whatever I needed as a child, she made sure I had," says Deion.

Even as a little boy, Deion loved sports. He played football, baseball, and basketball. Luckily for him, he had natural athletic ability. "I'm blessed," he explains.

Deion slugs a homer for the Yankees.

Deion was smart, as well. He understood
that if you want to be a great athlete, you have
to take care of your mind and body. "I have never
tasted alcohol," Deion says. "I have never tried
a cigarette in my life. I have never taken drugs."

When he was 12 years old, Deion was a
batboy for the Fort Myers Royals, a minor-league
baseball team run by the Kansas City Royals.
Batboys help out with equipment during games
and practices. Sometimes, they even get to play
catch with the players. Being a batboy was a
real thrill for young Deion. It inspired him to
work hard on his baseball skills.

Deion attended North Fort Myers High
School, where he was a star in three sports.
He was second-team All-State in basketball,
averaging 24 points per game during his senior
year. And he was so good at baseball that the
Kansas City Royals wanted him to sign a
professional contract. But Deion said no. He
wanted to go to college to play his best sport,

football. On the North Fort Myers High team, Deion played both offense and defense. He was the team's quarterback, passing for 839 yards and rushing for 499 as a senior. He also was a star defensive back.

Defensive backs have a hard job. When the other team's quarterback passes the ball, defensive backs try to stop the receivers from making catches. Sometimes, defensive backs get into position and intercept the pass. So to defend against the pass, a defensive back needs great speed, fine balance, and keen instincts. A defensive back must also respond when the offense runs the ball. Then, the defense must fend off blocks and make tackles. This calls for a lot of agility and strength. Deion had all these skills. He was both speedy and powerful, and he had a terrific instinct for intercepting passes. It's no wonder that college football teams were interested in having Deion play for them.

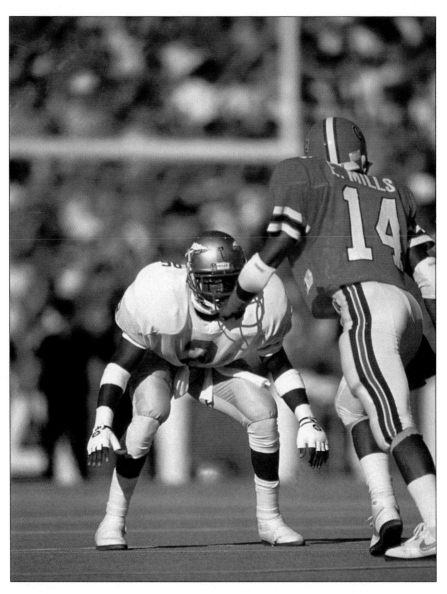

As soon as he joined the Florida State Seminoles, Deion was
a big star.

Deion decided to attend Florida State University, which had one of the best football programs in the country. In his freshman year, 1985, he played in almost every game for the Seminoles. Against Tulsa, he intercepted a pass on his own team's goal line and ran it back 100 yards for a touchdown. That broke the school record for longest interception return. After the regular season, Florida State played in the Gator Bowl against Oklahoma State. In the big game, Deion made six tackles and had an interception. The Seminoles won the game, 34-23.

After his exciting freshman football season, Deion switched sports. He played just as well for Florida State's baseball team. He hit .333 with 11 stolen bases.

★ ★ ★

In 1986, people began recognizing Deion's unique abilities. In football, he made *The Sporting News* first-team All-America squad. In baseball, he stole 28 bases as the Seminoles made it to the College World Series. In addition to all that, Deion added a new sport — track and field.

Deion had never competed in track before. He was such a fast runner that many people encouraged him to give it a try. Between baseball games, Deion ran on the 400-meter relay team.

In his junior year, Deion had an amazing football season. Playing cornerback, Deion was named a consensus All-American. Football announcer Brent Musburger said Sanders was the "best cornerback in the country and as fine a punt returner as I've seen." With Deion's help, the Seminoles beat Nebraska in the Fiesta Bowl, 31-28. They ended the season ranked second in the country.

Deion decided not to play baseball during his junior year. Instead, he competed in track — with incredible results. Deion placed first in the 100-meter and 200-meter dashes at the Metro Conference championships. Then, he ran on the winning 400-meter relay team. He was voted MVP for the meet.

Florida State track coach Dick Roberts was astounded by Deion's performance. "I don't believe in my experience in track and field, which spans 23 years, that I have ever been associated with, or witnessed, anyone that performed so well, so quickly," Roberts said.

But Deion had not put baseball behind him forever. In the summer between his junior and senior years in college, the New York Yankees offered Deion a contract. If he signed the contract, he would never be allowed to play college baseball again. Still, Deion was confident enough in his ability that he decided to give pro baseball a try.

Deion played in the outfield for three of the Yankees' minor-league teams that summer and showed great potential. "I wouldn't put any limitations on what he is capable of doing," said one of his managers.

Even though he had played professional baseball, Deion was still allowed to play football for Florida State. And Deion had an outstanding senior season. He was the national punt return champion. He averaged an impressive 15.2 yards per return.

In a game against Clemson, Florida State trailed 14-7 when Deion got ready to field a punt. "Watch out!" he shouted to the Clemson players. "This one's coming back!" True to his word, Deion ran the ball back 76 yards for a touchdown. The Seminoles won the game by three points.

At Florida State, Deion became feared on the football field. He was dangerous on defense, and he also returned several punts for touchdowns.

Deion began his NFL career in 1989 as an Atlanta Falcon. He was a big success from the start.

Led by Deion, the Florida State Seminoles had a great year. They finished the regular season with a 10-1 record. Then they played Auburn in the Sugar Bowl in front of a huge national television audience. The game came down to the final few seconds. With Florida State holding a slim lead, Auburn tried to pass for a touchdown to tie the game. But Deion made a dramatic interception to give his team the win.

After the season, Deion again was named a consensus All-American. He also won the Jim Thorpe Award as the best defensive back in college football. It was a fitting honor. Thorpe was one of the greatest American athletes of this century. He played both pro football and pro baseball — something that very few other athletes had been able to accomplish in the years since. But now, it looked like Deion might be able to follow in Thorpe's footsteps.

After the college football season ended, Deion was selected in the first round of the NFL draft by the Atlanta Falcons. Deion hoped to play football in the fall, but he also wanted to play baseball. In the spring of 1989, he joined the Yankees' AA minor-league team. The Yankees were impressed by Deion's play. After only 33 games, he was called up to the big leagues.

Suddenly, Deion found himself playing center field in Yankee Stadium. Legends such as Mickey Mantle and Joe DiMaggio had played the same position in the same, historic stadium. "I couldn't believe it. I'm thinking about Mickey Mantle, and about Babe Ruth and Lou Gehrig. I'm saying, 'I'm 21 years old and I'm really here,' " he remembers.

Deion had trouble hitting major-league pitching. He hit only .212. So he spent the rest of the season between the Yankees and their top minor-league team. "There's no doubt in my mind that he can become a major-league star," Yankee owner George Steinbrenner predicted at the time. "Sure, he made some mistakes, but those are of a learning-experience type. I've never seen a kid come in and do what he did."

Deion is so fast that he can usually outrun the receiver he is guarding.

Deion had to end his baseball season early to play football for the Falcons. His amazing, 68-yard punt return for a touchdown against the Rams got his NFL career off to a great start. But Deion didn't let up. In his first year with the team, Deion had five interceptions and many other great plays. In one play, he tackled Rams receiver Ron Brown to stop a touchdown. Brown was a very fast runner. He had been a member of the U.S. Olympic team. But on the football field, Deion was even faster than the Olympian. Deion caught Brown from behind!

"I've never seen a guy with such athletic ability," said one Falcon coach.

Many people predicted that Deion would give up baseball now that he had proven himself on the football field. But Deion had no intention of retiring from baseball. In the summer of 1990, he returned to the Yankees.

Deion was becoming one of the most famous athletes in America. But not all of his reputation was based on his athletic success. Some of it was due to the fancy clothes and jewelry that he always wore. Some of it also came from the huge amount of money that he earned. And a lot of it came from Deion's outgoing, self-assured personality. For instance, when Deion scored a touchdown, he would do a special dance when he reached the end zone. Deion was so confident about his own abilities that he called himself "Prime Time."

From the start of his pro career, Deion has been the center of attention.

In 1990, many fans were comparing Deion to Bo Jackson. Jackson was the only other modern athlete to succeed in both pro baseball and pro football. He played for the Los Angeles Raiders in football and the Kansas City Royals in baseball.

Deion once called Bo "one of the best athletes to ever put on a uniform." But just a few months later, tragedy struck Jackson's career. Bo hurt his hip while playing for the Raiders. The injury was so serious that Bo had to retire from football. After major surgery on his hip, Bo came back and played baseball. But he was not the same player as before the injury, and he retired from pro sports in 1994.

No doubt, Deion Sanders was watching Bo Jackson's comeback with great interest. Many people worried that Deion might suffer a career-threatening injury if he kept playing two sports. But Deion insisted on competing in both baseball and football.

With the heaving hitting in football, players are always at risk of serious injury. People wondered if Deion would quit football to preserve his health for baseball.

Deion joined the Atlanta Braves in 1991.

During the 1990 NFL season, Deion played even better than he had in his rookie year. He had 50 tackles, two fumble recoveries, and three interceptions, including one that he returned 82 yards for a touchdown against the Houston Oilers. He also returned a punt 79 yards for a touchdown against the Cincinnati Bengals. It was the longest punt return in Falcons history.

When the 1991 baseball season began, Deion was with a new team. The Yankees had grown tired of losing Deion to football every August. He left the team early every season to join the Falcons. So the Yankees released Deion, but the Atlanta Braves were glad to offer him a contract.

The Braves were a team on the rise. With great young pitchers like Tom Glavine and John Smoltz, they needed to bolster their offense. Deion, however, was having trouble at the plate. The Braves had to send him to the minor leagues for part of the season.

Time in the minors turned Deion around.
When he came back to the Braves, he began
to contribute. On July 31, 1991, Deion hit a
dramatic, three-run home run to help the Braves
beat the Pittsburgh Pirates. After the game,
however, he had to say goodbye to his teammates.
The Falcons' practice season was beginning, and
Deion had to resume his football career.

But Deion's departure from the Braves didn't
last long. Two months later, the Braves were
in a close race for first place in the National
League West against the Los Angeles Dodgers.
The Braves asked Deion if he could play for
them and the Falcons at the same time. He
decided to give it a try.

He finished the baseball season with the
Braves while continuing to play football on
Sundays for the Falcons. It was the first time
in the history that a player had competed in
two pro sports at the same time.

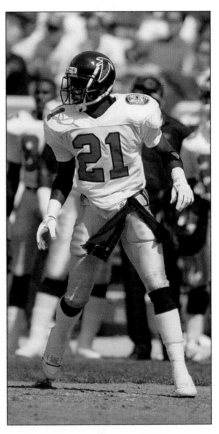

In 1991, Deion was a two-sport star in Atlanta. He played football (right) for the Falcons and baseball (left) for the Braves.

Teammates give Deion a hand during the Pro Bowl.

The Braves won the National League pennant in 1991, making it to the World Series. There, they lost to the Minnesota Twins. Deion didn't see any playing time during the Series. Still, he was happy to be part of a pennant-winning team.

As soon as the World Series ended, Deion continued his great football season. He collected six interceptions and one fumble recovery. He also returned a kickoff 100 yards for a touchdown against the San Francisco 49ers. And for the first time in his career, Deion was named to play in the Pro Bowl, the NFL's all-star game. It was a great honor.

Despite his football accomplishments, Deion was not satisfied. He wanted to improve his baseball skills. He wanted to become an everyday player, not just an occasional starter. As the 1992 baseball season approached, he said, "I've been focusing on nothing but baseball. I never approached baseball with the attitude that I did in my other sport — that I could be a star."

Deion opened the season with a 14-game hitting streak. He hit .304 for the season. He also led the National League with 14 triples. The Braves did well, too. They finished in first place.

In the playoffs, Deion again made history. On October 11, 1992, he played football for the Falcons in Miami against the Dolphins, then flew to Pittsburgh in time for that night's baseball game. It was the first time a pro athlete had suited up for teams in different sports on the same day.

A helicopter carrying Deion arrives in Pittsburgh on October 11, 1992. Deion had played a football game in Miami that day. He flew to Pittsburgh to join the Braves for the baseball playoffs the same night.

In 1994, Deion was traded to the Cincinnati Reds.

The Braves made it to the 1992 World Series, but lost again — this time to the Toronto Blue Jays. This time, however, Deion got to play, and he played his heart out. He hit .533 and stole five bases.

By 1994, Deion was frustrated. He was a star in two sports, but he had never won a championship in either. And his frustrations increased during the 1994 baseball season. First, Deion was traded from the Braves to the Cincinnati Reds. Then, a strike by the players ended the season prematurely.

The crowd goes wild as Deion scores a touchdown on an interception.

After the 1993-94 football season, Deion was a free agent. Several teams offered him contracts. He chose the San Francisco 49ers. "They are a first-class organization," Deion said. "I know they are going to win. They have a lot of superstars on the team. All the focus and all the pressure isn't on me. I can just be a regular guy."

The 49ers were a good team, but Deion helped make them great. He had an amazing season, intercepting six passes and returning three for touchdowns. The Associated Press named Deion the NFL Defensive Player of the Year.

The 49ers also had an incredible year, finishing the regular season with a record of 13-3. Their first opponent in the NFC playoffs was the Chicago Bears. San Francisco won that game easily, 44-15. The Bears were so afraid of Deion's defensive skills that they never even threw a pass in his direction!

In the NFC title game, the 49ers played the Super Bowl champion Dallas Cowboys. Deion had a great game, and the 49ers won, 38-28.

In the Super Bowl, San Francisco went up against the San Diego Chargers. It wasn't even close. The 49ers triumphed by a score of 49-26. Deion Sanders was finally a champion!

At Super Bowl XXIX in 1995, Deion became a champion in the NFL.

After capturing Super Bowl glory, Deion changed uniforms once again. He signed a multi-year contract for the Dallas Cowboys as the 1995-96 season began.

And what about baseball? Is a World Series title next for the two-sport superstar? It's hard to tell. Deion was traded to the San Francisco Giants in 1995, but the team struggled through a poor season. As the baseball season ended, some people believed he would retire from baseball. Deion had been hinting that he wanted to spend more time with his wife, Carolyn, and his two children, Deiondra and Deion, Jr.

"The family means more than everything to me," explains Deion. "That's why I don't care what people say about me when I'm done with the game. People always ask the question, 'What do you want people to say about you when it's all over?' I don't want them to say [anything]. I want my kids to say: 'Daddy is a good father. He provided, helped us with our homework, taught us values.' That's what I want."

Deion joined the Dallas Cowboys in 1995.

C ★ H ★ R ★ O ★ N

1967 • August 9: Deion Luwynn Sanders is born in Fort Myers, Florida.

1981-85 • Deion attends North Fort Myers High School, where he stars in baseball, basketball, and football.

1985-86 • As a freshman at Florida State University, Deion earns All-American status as a football player; in baseball, he hits .333 with 11 stolen bases.

1986-87 • Deion is named All-American in football.

1987-88 • In track, Deion is named Most Valuable Player of the Metro Conference championship meet. Deion does not play college baseball, but signs with the New York Yankees and plays for three of the Yankees' minor-league teams.

O ★ L ★ O ★ G ★ Y

1989-90 • The Atlanta Falcons select Deion in the first round of the college draft. In September 1988, Deion becomes the fist athlete to hit a major-league home run and score an NFL touchdown in the same week.

1990-91 • Deion signs with the Atlanta Braves. In football, he is named to the 1991 NFC Pro Bowl team.

1991-92 • Playing for the Atlanta Braves, Deion hits .533 with five stolen bases in the 1992 World Series.

1993-94 • Deion makes the 1993 Pro Bowl, his third consecutive year. In baseball, he is traded from the Braves to the Cincinnati Reds.

1994-95 • Deion plays for the San Francisco 49ers, who win the 1995 Super Bowl.

1995-96 • In baseball, Deion is traded from the Cincinnati Reds to the San Francisco Giants; in football, he signs with the Dallas Cowboys.

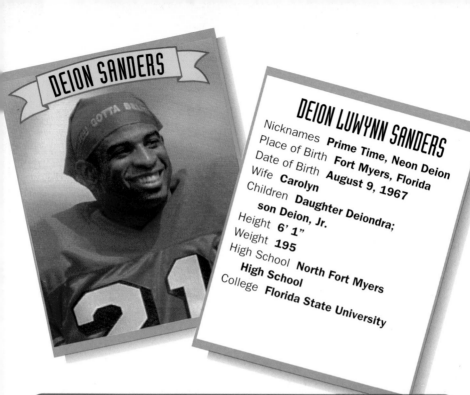

DEION SANDERS

DEION LUWYNN SANDERS

Nicknames **Prime Time, Neon Deion**
Place of Birth **Fort Myers, Florida**
Date of Birth **August 9, 1967**
Wife **Carolyn**
Children **Daughter Deiondra;
son Deion, Jr.**
Height **6' 1"**
Weight **195**
High School **North Fort Myers
High School**
College **Florida State University**

⭐ MAJOR-LEAGUE BASEBALL ⭐

	Batting Average	Home Runs	Runs	Stolen Bases
Career Totals	.264	33	249	127

(New York Yankees, 1989-90; Atlanta Braves, 1991-94; Cincinnati Reds, 1994-95; San Francisco Giants, 1995)

⭐ PRO FOOTBALL ⭐

	Games	Interceptions	Touchdowns
Career Totals	84	30	13

(Atlanta Falcons, 1989-93; San Francisco 49ers, 1993-94)

47

⭐ ⭐ ⭐

About the Author

Miles Harvey is a journalist who has worked for *In These Times* and United Press International. He is the author of several books for Children's Press, including biographies of Barry Bonds, Juan Gonzalez, and Hakeem Olajuwon. Mr. Harvey lives in Chicago, where he watches a lot of sports with his good buddy, Dick Cohen.